MOOMINMAMMA'S
book of thoughts

ILLUSTRATIONS AND QUOTATIONS BY TOVE JANSSON
TEXT BY SAMI MALILA
TRANSLATION BY PAMELA KASKINEN

SELF
MADE
HERO

Excerpts and illustrations by Tove Jansson © Moomin Characters Ltd., Finland
Text © Sami Malila and WSOY
Original title: "Muumimamman mietekirja"
First published in Finnish by Werner Söderström Corporation (WSOY) in 2003,
Helsinki, Finland
Translation into English © Pamela Kaskinen
First published in English by SelfMadeHero in 2010
A division of Metro Media Ltd
5 Upper Wimpole Street London W1G 6BP
www.selfmadehero.com

Publishing Director: Emma Hayley
Marketing Director: Doug Wallace
Layout designer: Kurt Young
With thanks to: Nick de Somogyi and Jane Laporte

This work has been published with the financial assistance of
FILI– Finnish Literature Exchange

FILI
FINNISH LITERATURE EXCHANGE

A CIP record for this book is available from the British Library

978-1-906838-18-8

10 9 8 7 6 5 4 3 2

Printed and bound in England

To the Reader

THE BELOVED MOOMIN STORIES OF
TOVE JANSSON ARE FULL OF THRILLING
ADVENTURES, EXUBERANT HUMOUR, ETERNAL
TRUTHS AND TIMELESS WISDOM.

AS THE MATRON OF THE MOOMIN FAMILY,
MOOMINMAMMA KEEPS A WARM AND COSY
HOME THAT IS A SAFE HAVEN FOR BOTH FRIENDS
AND PASSERS-BY. THIS BOOK IS A COLLECTION OF
MOOMINMAMMA'S THOUGHTS ON FRIENDSHIP,
COURAGE AND UNDERSTANDING. THEY OFFER A
GLIMPSE OF MAMMA'S ABIDING SERENITY AND
HER UNIQUE ABILITY TO ALWAYS SEE THE
SILVER LINING, EVEN IN DISASTER.

WE HOPE YOU ENJOY THE WISE WORDS AND
ENCHANTING INSIGHTS OF MOOMINMAMMA'S
BOOK OF THOUGHTS!

Excerpts and illustrations are from the following WSOY editions of the Moomin books, translated from the original Swedish into Finnish:

MUUMIPEIKKO JA PYRSTÖTÄHTI

TAIKURIN HATTU

VAARALLINEN JUHANNUS

TAIKATALVI

NÄKYMÄTÖN LAPSI JA MUITA KERTOMUKSIA

MUUMIPAPAN UROTYÖT

MUUMIPAPPA JA MERI

MUUMILAAKSON MARRASKUU

Contents

Everyday Life 6

Friendship and Caring 14

Moominmamma's Pearls of Wisdom 18

Simple Joys 24

Freedom and Equality 32

Dear Moominmamma 38

Love 42

Everyday Life

SUDDENLY the house was filled with activity; there was the sound of slamming doors and shouting. Moominmamma ran in holding a candle.

"Oh thank goodness, it was only you!" she said. "I thought some kind of villain had broken in!"

"I just wanted to get the palm-tree wine down," said Moominpappa. "But some fool put this stupid platter where it was bound to fall."

"Well, never mind. It was pretty ugly to begin with," said Moominmamma.

"MY darling child, something terrible has happened!" cried Moominmamma. "My handbag has gone missing! I simply cannot manage without it! I've looked everywhere and it is nowhere to be found!"

Everyone joined in a massive search. Only the Muskrat refused to participate.

"Of all of the useless things in the world, handbags are

without a doubt the most useless," the Muskrat said.

"Time will pass and the days will change, the same as ever, regardless of whether Moomimamma finds her handbag or not."

"Yes, but one thing will be entirely different!" said Moominpappa, indignant. "Moominmamma will seem like a total stranger without her handbag. Why, I've never seen her without it!"

AFTER the meal was finished (it wasn't very tasty, I'm afraid), they all wished each other a sincere and heartfelt "goodnight". Moominmamma reminded everyone to brush their teeth well and Moominpappa walked through the house and shut all the doors and fastened all the windows. He hung a drape over the chandelier so it wouldn't gather dust.

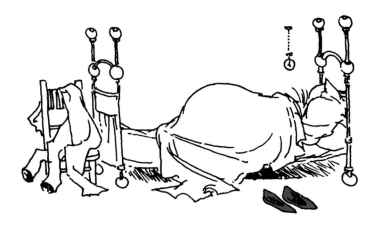

"MAMMA!" yelled Moomintroll, "Come and look at Pappa!"

Moominmamma opened the kitchen door and paused at the threshold in surprise.

"Well? Does it suit me?" asked Moominpappa.

"Why yes, it does," said Moominmamma. "You look very manly. It is a trifle too big, though, don't you think?"

"How about now? Is this better?" asked Moominpappa, pushing the hat back from his forehead.

"Hmm," said Moominmamma. "It is very nice indeed. But I think you look even more dignified without a hat."

Moominpappa looked at his reflection in the mirror and examined himself from all sides. Then he placed the hat on the dresser with a sigh.

"You're right," he said. "Some people just don't need any finery."

"Men are most handsome when they're healthy," said Moominmamma warmly.

MOOMINMAMMA sat on the roof, cradling her handbag, a sewing basket, a coffee pot and the family photo album in her lap. She moved from time to time to avoid the rising flood water because she preferred not to get her tail wet, particularly now that they had company.

"There is no way we can rescue everything," said Moominpappa.

"Dearest Pappa," said Mamma. "What's the use of tables without chairs and chairs without tables? And what good is a bed with no linen closet?"

MOOMINPAPPA rose to gather his papers, insulted.

"If you don't like the play I wrote, then by all means write one of your own," he said.

"Oh no, no, we all thought it was just wonderful, darling," said Moominmamma. "Isn't that right?"

"Yes, yes, of course," everyone nodded eagerly.

"You just wait and see," said Mamma. "It will be a smashing success as soon as you change the plot a bit and make a few corrections to the writing style. I'll see to it that no one disturbs you while you work on the rewrite, and that the bowl of sweets will be right by your side."

"All right then, I suppose I could give it a try," said Moominpappa.

Friendship and Caring

SNIFF AND MOOMINTROLL HAD FALLEN ASLEEP ON
THE RUG IN THE MIDDLE OF THE PARLOUR FLOOR.
MOOMINMAMMA SPREAD A BLANKET OVER THEM
AND THEN SAT DOWN BY THE WINDOW TO MEND
PAPPA'S NIGHTSHIRT.

JUST as all this was taking place, Moominmamma was walking around the house feeling exceedingly pleased. The rain fell quietly in the garden and a sense of peace, order and tranquillity was in the air.

"Everything is sure to grow now!" said Moominmamma to herself, blissfully. "It is so wonderful that the children are safe at the cave!"

"BUT why would they be feuding with each other if they are related?" asked Moominmamma cautiously. "And aren't there any princesses in the play? Can't there be a happy ending? Death is so depressing."

"But it is a tragic play, my dear," replied Moominpappa. "That means that someone has to die at the end."

MOOMINMAMMA went straight to the kitchen to prepare some warm blackcurrant juice.

"Sorry about the dirty dishes," yelled Moomintroll contritely from the next room.

"All in good time," said his mother. "Don't worry yourself now."

She found some kindling behind the rubbish pail and then went to her secret cupboard and took out some currant-juice concentrate. She also located some medicinal powder and a flannel scarf.

Moominmamma's Pearls of Wisdom

"IT just goes to show you," said Mamma thoughtfully, as she squinted up towards the sun. "Life is truly curious. Just when I thought I had seen it all and was convinced that the silver platter could only be used for one purpose, along comes an entirely better use for it. And to think that every season people tell me that I make far too much jam and now every last bit of it has been eaten!"

"HOW odd that an exceedingly agreeable life could make us depressed or irritated. But that's the way it is. It seems to me that the best thing for it is to start again from the beginning."

"GOOD gracious," said Moominmamma. "What a scene I have managed to create!" But she had to admit she was secretly very pleased about the whole thing.

MOOMINMAMMA laughed with pleasure. "That's right, Misabel was happy. Now she can act in tragic plays for the rest of her life, with a new costume every time. And Whomper is the new stage manager and every bit as happy as Misabel. Isn't it wonderful when friends manage to live their lives just as they would like to?"

"It certainly is," said Moomintroll. "Wonderful indeed."

"THAT is going to be our new home," Moominmamma repeated. "It is Pappa's island. He will look after all of us there. We are going to move there and live there as long as there is life in us. We are going to start everything afresh, right from the beginning."

"I've always thought that it was just a speck of dirt on the horizon," said Little My.

Moominmamma climbed back down. "Sometimes you just need time," she continued quietly. "At times it may seem as if the wait is unbearable... until you finally understand." Then she got up and went to the garden.

THEY clambered from one grey and creviced precipice to another.

"Everything here is so large, somehow," thought Moominmamma. "Or else it is me that is too small."

Simple Joys

MOOMINTROLL'S FACE COLOURED WITH SHAME.
"SO LITTLE MY TOLD YOU?" HE ASKED.
"YES, SHE DID," SAID MOOMINMAMMA.
"IT SEEMS I OWE YOU A DEBT OF GRATITUDE FOR
TAKING SUCH GOOD CARE OF OUR GUESTS. NOW
THERE IS NO REASON FOR ME TO FEEL BAD ABOUT
OUR POOR HOSPITALITY. YOU KNOW, I HAVE TO SAY
THAT THE HOUSE SEEMS MUCH AIRIER WITHOUT ALL
OF THOSE EXTRA RUGS AND TRINKETS — AND NOW
WE WON'T NEED TO CLEAN SO OFTEN."

MOOMINMAMMA found a sheltered spot from the wind and nestled inside. From here, she could only see the blue sky and the coastal flowers swaying in the wind above her. "I'll just rest here for a moment," she thought to herself. But she soon fell fast asleep in the warm sand.

"I need something to fortify me," said the Hobgoblin. "This whole matter is making me most upset."

Moominmamma ran to get some pancakes and jam and a large plate. As the Hobgoblin ate, everyone dared to move in closer. After all, anyone who eats pancakes and jam can't be too dangerous. You can talk to someone like that.

"No dishes to wash today!" said Moominmamma with glee. "Perhaps I will never ever have to wash them again."

OF course, they did have an awful lot of things to do at dusk. They were always scurrying around. By and by Moominmamma would go down into the cellar to fetch some sausages or butter for tea. Or work in the potato patch. Or gather firewood. Each time it looked as if she sought out a strange new route to her destination, which was very exciting. But you never quite knew for sure. She could have been out on a secret errand of her own, amusing herself, or simply walking around for the sake of it, feeling very much alive.

MOOMINMAMMA didn't say anything. She padded back and forth, arranging things before bedtime, just as she had always done in the evening. She searched for something in her handbag and then turned the lamp down. All the while there was an eerie silence in the room. Finally she began absent-mindedly to wipe the dust from Pappa's model lighthouse sitting on the corner shelf.

MOOMINMAMMA had long since found the proper place for all of the things that they had brought along from their home in Moominvalley. There was no need for her to do much cleaning, for there was little dust this far out to sea and she didn't consider cleanliness such an important virtue anyway. As for the meals, she prepared them quickly, with a carefree spirit.

MOOMINMAMMA was peaceful and content. She dreamed of carrots, radishes and potatoes growing fat and round in the warm sunshine. She could see healthy green leaves sprouting, strong and succulent. She imagined the stalks heavy with tomatoes, peas and beans, swaying in the wind against the background of the blue sea. They would provide food for her family.

freedom and Equality

"WHERE have you been?" asked Moominpappa, all flustered.

"Me?" Mamma replied innocently. "Oh, I just went for a little stroll to get some air."

"You musn't go about frightening us like that," said Pappa. "Keep in mind that we are used to having you around the house in the evenings."

"That's just the trouble, isn't it," sighed Moominmamma. "It is good to have a change once in a while and yet we grow so accustomed to each other and expect everything to stay the same. Isn't that right, dear?"

MOOMINMAMMA laughed. Then she said thoughtfully, "As long as we have been out here on this island, I have had this feeling as if we have been on an extended outing. I mean, everything is different in a new, exciting way. It is almost as if every day was Sunday. I wonder if it might be wrong to feel this way."

The others waited in silence.

"You see, life can't be just one continuous outing," Mamma continued hesitantly. "It has to end sometime. I'm afraid that soon every day will start to feel like a Monday and then I shan't be able to believe all this has been real…" She broke off and looked hesitantly at Moominpappa.

"JACARANDA and palisander wood," murmured Moominmamma contentedly and continued with her sawing.

The others had got used to Mamma and her sawing; they could see less and less of her, behind the rising piles of wood. At first Moominpappa insisted that he take over, but then Mamma became cross and said, "No, this is my place, my job. I want to play, too."

MOOMINMAMMA found herself thinking: "What if the island came loose? All of sudden we could be rippling in the water right there by our very own pier back home. Imagine if we drifted even further, sailing for years until the island toppled right off the edge of the world, like a coffee cup on a slippery tray…"

"LITTLE My would like that," thought Mamma, and giggled to herself. "I wonder where she sleeps at night. Or Moomintroll for that matter… What a pity mothers can't just pick up and leave whenever they want and sleep out of doors. It is mothers in particular that could really do with it sometimes."

"ARE you sad about something?" Moominmamma asked.

"No," answered Moomintroll.

"Tomorrow is a fresh new day, remember," said Mamma. "And it'll be all yours, from beginning to end. Now isn't that a happy thought?"

ONCE upon a time, long ago, Moominpappa left home with no explanation and without understanding himself what had compelled him to leave.

Moominmamma said later that Pappa had been acting peculiar for some time, but it is doubtful that his behaviour was any more odd than usual. These kinds of justifications are usually invented afterwards, when people are bewildered and sad and in need of an explanation that brings them comfort.

"HE'LL be back in due course," said Moominmamma. "He was clear from the start. He has always returned in the past, so he is bound to do so again."

No one was worried, which was a good thing. They had decided never to worry about each other, so no one had a bad conscience and everyone could enjoy as much freedom as possible.

Dear Moominmamma

MOOMINTROLL PULLED HIS MATTRESS
DOWN AND LAID IT NEXT TO HIS
MOTHER'S BED. MOOMINMAMMA SIGHED
IN HER SLEEP, MUMBLING SOMETHING
UNINTELLIGIBLE. SHE THEN CHUCKLED
IN HER DREAMS AND ROLLED TOWARDS
THE WALL.

MOOMINMAMMA sighed and turned over. Moomintroll whispered yet again.

She answered in her sleep. The reply rose from deep inside her, revealing her innate womanly knowledge of tradition. "The black ribbons for mourning... they are in my closet... top shelf... to the right..." And then she sank back into her deep winter sleep.

MOOMINMAMMA gathered some snow in her paws and made a snowball. Her throwing technique was all wrong, like with so many mothers, and her snowball fell to the ground just a short distance from where she stood.

"I guess I'm not much good at that," she said, laughing.

MOOMINTROLL watched Moominmamma toss and turn for a while on her damp mattress until she found a comfy position. Then she sighed and fell asleep. Of all of the events that had taken place, this was without a doubt the most extraordinary. Mamma had fallen asleep in a new place without unpacking, without first making up the beds for the others and without distributing any sweets. She had even left her handbag behind on the sand. Her behaviour was alarming, but at the same time it was exhilarating. It signified that this was no mere adventure: this was going to be a real change.

"Hush, children," said Moominpappa. "No need to make a fuss. Moominmamma can choose the name. This is her adventure, after all."

Moominmamma blushed.

"I doubt I could think of a very good one," she said shyly. "Snufkin has plenty of imagination. I'm certain he could think of a better one."

"If I must, dears," said Moominmamma. "Only you musn't think I'm silly or old-fashioned. I believe the name of the boat should remind us of what we plan to do with it. I think we should call her *The Adventure*."

"Wonderful!" yelled Moomintroll. "Let's christen her right away!"

Love

DUSK had fallen. Suddenly Pappa's crystal ball changed and began shining brightly. Moominmamma had lit the oil lamp on the veranda, the first time this summer. It was as if the feeling of safety was suddenly concentrated at one single point alone: that little veranda. There Mamma sat, waiting for her family to return home so she could put the kettle on for their evening tea.

"WHAT'S wrong?" asked Moominmamma.

The room was blue and quiet; the dark night could be seen from each of its four windows.

"I had a dream," said Moominpappa. "It was awful."

Mamma got up and put a few pieces of dry wood on the glowing ashes of the fire. They lit quickly and the warm yellow light flickered in the darkness.

"I'll make you a sandwich," said Mamma. "This is a new place, after all."

Moominpappa sat on the edge of his bed and ate his sandwich. Gradually, his fear dissipated.

"THE sound of the sea is really rather nice,"
said Moominmamma, pulling the blanket up past her chin.
"It's different. Are you sure you won't have more bad
dreams now?"

"I doubt it," answered Moominpappa. "Sandwiches
always seem to do the trick in the middle of the night."

"Mamma," called Moomintroll, "is it all over now?"

"Yes, my darling Moomin child, it's over," answered his mother. "Everything is back to normal and you can go to sleep. Don't cry, Sniff, the danger has passed."

The Snork Maiden was trembling. "That was simply dreadful!"

"And I didn't even get an orange," said the silk monkey.

"Maybe another time," Mamma answered. "I will sing you all a lullaby now, to help you fall asleep." And she began to sing:

Sleep little children, black is the night,
Comets will pass us by when the moment is right.
Slip into your dream worlds, forget about the rest.
Night has covered everything, and that is for the best.
The sun is hidden from us, everything is still.
The only creatures moving are the lambs upon the hill.

Slowly, one by one, they dropped off to sleep and quietness filled the cave.

The End